# Stop it, Billy!

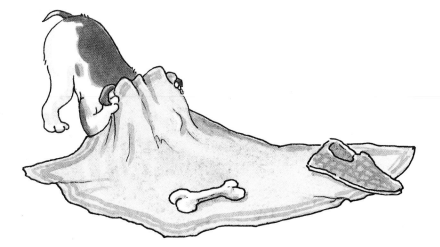

Nelson

2 two

"Stop it, Billy!" said Billy's Mum.

"I'll play it to Grandad," said Billy.

"Stop it, Billy!" said Grandad.

"I'll play it to Ruff," said Billy.

"I'll play it out here," said Billy.

9 nine

"Stop it, Billy!" said Max.

"Stop it, Billy!" said Magpie.

3

4

5

6

8